D0409309

PET

VICTORIAN LIFE

A VICTORIAN KITCHEN

LUCY FAULKNER

Wayland

VICTORIAN LIFE

HOW WE LEARN ABOUT THE VICTORIANS

Queen Victoria reigned from 1837 to 1901, a time when Britain went through enormous social and industrial changes. We can learn about Victorians in various ways.

We can still see many of their buildings standing today, we can look at their documents, maps and artefacts – many of which can be found in museums. Photography, invented during Victoria's reign, gives us a good picture of life in Victorian Britain. In this book you will see what Victorian life was like through some of this historical evidence.

Series design: Pardoe Blacker Ltd
Editor: Sarah Doughty

First published in 1994 by Wayland (Publishers) Ltd, 61 Western Road, Hove, East Sussex BN3 1JD, England

© Copyright 1994 Wayland (Publishers) Ltd

British Library Cataloguing in Publication Data
Faulkner, Lucy. – (Victorian Kitchen)
 I. Title II. Series
 641.50941

ISBN 0 7502 1159 8

Printed and bound in Great Britain by B.P.C.C. Paulton Books Ltd

CITY OF COVENTRY SCHOOLS LIBRARY SERVICE LIBRARY

Cover picture: A Victorian cottage kitchen.

Picture acknowledgements: BBC Enterprises 18 (both); Bridgeman Art Library *cover*, 4, 8, 11, 14 (bottom), 22; E.T Archive 9 (bottom), 17 (bottom); Eye Ubiquitous 27 (bottom); Mary Evans Picture Library 5 (bottom), 13, 14 (top), 15 (bottom), 20, 24; John Frost's Historical Newspapers 9 (top); Hulton-Deutsch Collection 10 (top); Billie Love Collection 10 (bottom), 23 (bottom), 25 (top); Mansell Collection 25 (bottom); National Trust Photographic Library 7 (Andreas von Einsiedel), 12 (Rob Matheson), 23 top (Mark Fiennes); Norfolk Museums Service 7 (bottom); Robert Opie 17 (top), 26 (both); Popperfoto 6; Richard Wood 5 (top); Wayland Picture Library 15 (Leigh Goodsall).

With thanks to Norfolk Museums Service for supplying items from their museums on pages 16, 19, 21 (both), 27 (top). The commissioned photography is by GGS Photo Graphics

CONTENTS

KITCHEN EQUIPMENT

At the heart of the early Victorian kitchen was the cooking fire. What else do you think a kitchen needs? Many of the things that we think of as important kitchen equipment today were not found in the Victorian kitchen at all. Sometimes the pump or tap, the bread oven and cool storage were not even found indoors. But Victorians took their cooking seriously and by the end of the nineteenth century, water from taps, cookers with ovens and even simple refrigerators could be found in many houses.

COTTAGE KITCHENS

In small cottages like the one in the picture, the kitchen was the main living room. Most of family life went on near the fire, for warmth. All day, someone needed to be at hand to tend the fire. Cooking was not easy on an open fire as it was difficult to control the heat. The family had to live with soot and smoke and cooking smells.

In the homes of wealthy families, living rooms were far away from the smells, heat and noise made by the work of the kitchen.

Preserving jam in the kitchen.

THE KITCHEN PUMP

It was unusual to find a water supply in early Victorian kitchens. Country people who lived in cottages almost always had to carry water in buckets from the nearest well. To lighten their task they would collect rainwater for washing and cooking. In towns, people could buy water from a water-carrier or use the public fountains or pumps. Towards the end of the nineteenth century, more houses had piped water and drains, making kitchen tasks like preparing vegetables much easier.

A water pump in a kitchen.

THE BAKING OVEN

Bread, cakes and pies were often not cooked in the kitchen at all, but were baked in brick ovens. These ovens were built into the sides of fireplaces. In some country areas, the ovens were built outside and were used by the whole neighbourhood. Bundles of dry wood or furze (bushy plants like gorse) were burnt to ashes in the oven. The oven was then cleaned out and the bread cooked in the heat held by the bricks.

In towns, the women would take bread and cakes to the baker's shop and pay to have them baked.

Country baking in Warwickshire, 1872.

COAL-FIRED RANGES

In 1802, iron stoves called ranges were invented. However, until the middle of the nineteenth century, ranges were only put into the kitchens of wealthy people. A range burned so much coal and needed so much cleaning that there had to be plenty of servants to look after it. Cooks and kitchenmaids had to learn how to control the fire to bring the oven to the right heat. To tell if it was hot enough, they would put flour or paper on the oven floor and watch it change colour.

A coal-fired iron range.

This range at Charlecote Park in Warwickshire has a large roasting oven with double doors on the right and two other ovens on the left. A huge copper water boiler sits above the fire. A kitchenmaid had to get up at 6 o'clock every morning to clean the range. She would take out the ashes, then polish the black parts with black lead on a brush dipped in turpentine. The shiny steel parts had to be scoured and polished. Once a week she got up earlier to clean the sooty flues as well.

Charlecote Park kitchen range.

KITCHENERS

Small ranges, known as kitcheners, became popular in smaller houses from the 1850s. They were much cleaner than the old open hearths as the fire, ashes and smoke were all enclosed. It was safer to cook with several pans at once, and there was a built-in oven. Once they became popular, kitcheners were made by iron-workers all over the country. Unfortunately, not all makers were experts, so some kitcheners smoked or would not burn well.

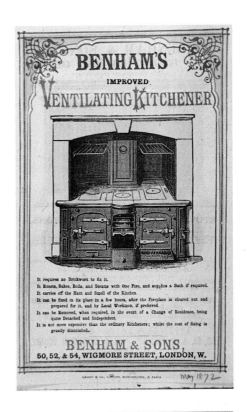

An advertisement for a kitchener, 1872.

KITCHEN WORKERS

How do you feel about doing the washing up? What about skinning a rabbit, scrubbing a stone floor on your hands and knees or cleaning sooty chimney pipes before breakfast? Kitchen work was much harder and more unpleasant than it is today. But for many girls, becoming a kitchen servant was their only choice if they were going to leave home and pay their way.

A poor woman cooking a meal.

KITCHEN WORK

For a woman with no servants to help her the work to be done in the kitchen was endless. There were no wipe-clean surfaces and the fire was constantly making dust and soot. Before anything else could be done, fuel and water had to be fetched. Without good lighting, many tasks had to be finished before night fell. It was hard work trying to feed yourself and the rest of the household when you had hardly any money to spend.

PLAIN AND PROFESSED COOKS

DOMESTIC SERVANTS WANTED.

A GOOD GENERAL SERVANT WANTED. Must understand plain cooking and be clean. Teetotaller preferred. Nursemaid kept. Wages £16 to commence, which would be quickly increased to a really capable and reliable girl.—Address W. H., Box 5,582, Postal Department, Daily Telegraph, Fleet-street, E.C.

A GOOD PLAIN COOK WANTED, by the 20th. Aged from 25 to 35. Must have good character. Wages £20. Also House-Parlourmaid, aged over 20. Must have good character. Wages £18. Four in family.—Apply at 5, Tavistock-road, Croydon.

A HOUSE BOY WANTED immediately, between 13 and 15.—Apply, before eleven or after six, at 7, Brunswick-gardens, Kensington.

A STRONG GIRL WANTED, for house and kitchen work. Good reference 6s. per week.—Apply at Three Crowns, Old Jewry, Cheapside, E.C.

A STRONG healthy young person WANTED, as GENERAL SERVANT, in a gentleman's private residence. Must understand plain cooking, and have good reference. Wages £12, all found.—Apply, in the first instance, at the George and Dragon, St. George's-road, Peckham (side door).

A YOUNG GIRL WANTED, as general servant.—Apply at Green Man, Berwick-street, Oxford-street.

AN experienced STILLROOM-MAID REQUIRED Under one kept.—Apply, with full particulars, at Calverley Hotel, Tunbridge-wells.

CAN a lady recommend a good COOK-HOUSEKEEPER to take charge of a small seaside house ? She would be alone and attend on the family when down from London during Easter and summer.—Apply by letter, stating wages required, to Mrs. C., 15, Sydenham-avenue.

CHILDREN'S MAID WANTED. Two children, ages four years and eight years. Comfortable home. Good wages.—Mrs. Pipe, 50, Edgware-road, Hyde Park.

COOK WANTED; also House-Parlourmaid. Good generals not objected. For elderly lady and gentleman. No family. Light place. Wages from £16 to £22.—Mrs. Pipe, 50, Edgware-road, Hyde Park.

COOK WANTED, £18 to £22; also House-Parlourmaid, £16 to £20. Only two in family. Comfortable situation.—Mrs. May, 26, Tottenham-court-road.

COOK-HOUSEKEEPER WANTED in boarding house. Four gentlemen boarders. No ladies; no children. Servant kept. Early rising, good cooking essential.—Apply to C. E. Lemaitre, Esq., 13, Coleherne-road, Earl's-court.

The most important job in the kitchen was, of course, cooking. There were two kinds of cook working in Victorian households. Plain cooks had probably learned cooking while working as kitchenmaids. Professed cooks were properly trained. They expected to have other servants to help them and would do only the more difficult cooking tasks. Plain cooks had to do other jobs such as cleaning the dining room and answering the door. By 1860 it was usual to advertise for a job as a cook, if no one could find a place for you by word of mouth.

Advertisements from the *Daily Telegraph*, 1895.

SERVANTS

Servants started work young, maybe aged 11. They would not earn much at first but they were fed and would learn the work. Girls like this teenager would start as scullerymaids or maids-of-all-work in small households. If they were good at their job they could become kitchenmaids and then cooks. The best job of all which an experienced cook could hope for was to be a cook-housekeeper. Servants often moved from place to place trying to better themselves. But most servant girls hoped to escape their life of service by marrying.

Peeling potatoes in the scullery.

THE HOUSEKEEPER

In big households the lower servants like kitchenmaids and scullerymaids might never speak to the mistress of the house. Where there was a housekeeper, she would give all orders and see the work was done properly. The housekeeper would do certain cooking jobs, like making jams, ice-cream, sponge cake and special puddings. Here she is on the left of the picture watching two of the kitchenmaids making pastry while the other servant collects dishes. Unlike the lower servants, the housekeeper did not have to wear a uniform. She had her own sitting-room and expected to be spoken to respectfully.

Housekeeper and servants, 1878.

THE MISTRESS'S ORDERS

A mistress giving instructions to a new cook.

Every morning a mistress would speak to her cook to give orders for meals and keep a check on how much was being spent. Cooks knew how important their work was and could make life difficult for their employers by threatening to leave. Cooks expected certain privileges to go with the job, for example, being able to sell the dripping from roasts, the used tea-leaves from the pot and rabbit skins. Sometimes employers put up with a cook's bad habits, such as drinking too much, because it was difficult to find a cook who was really good at the job.

MALE CHEFS

In the very grandest houses and hotels a male chef might be employed. Queen Victoria had a French chef with 24 others working under him. Employers sometimes complained that chefs were moody and difficult to work with. If their employer did not like what they had cooked the chef would leave. A French chef worked for the Duke of Wellington, the general who was famous for his defeat of Napoleon. His chef, Felix, left complaining that the Duke did not say anything, good or bad, about the remarkable dishes that he had prepared for him.

The kitchen of a large house.

A SERVANT'S DAY

Almost all of a kitchen servant's day would be spent in the gloom of a basement kitchen and the larders and sculleries alongside it. For servants, work was not just a part of life, it was nearly the whole of it. Even if a well-organized cook or kitchenmaid found herself with a little time to spare she would not be free to go out. It was never long until the next meal had to be prepared for the dining-room, servants' hall or nursery.

A clock on the wall at Saltram, Devon.

DAILY ROUTINE

The cook's day was ruled by the clock. Everyone else in the kitchen was ruled by the cook. This is how the day might go starting at 7 o'clock in the morning:

7.00	Bake rolls, prepare hot dishes for breakfast
7.45	Put on clean apron, go to prayers
8.00	Send up breakfast
8.15	Servants' breakfast
9.15	See mistress for orders
9.30	Prepare soups for next day
10.30	Prepare jellies and creams for next day and tarts for dinner
12.00	Servants' dinner

1.00	Send up luncheon and nursery dinner
2.00	Rest
3.00	Do accounts
4.00	Nursery tea
5.00	Start preparing dinner, send up tea
8.00	Send up dinner
9.00	Servants' supper

10.00	Close the fire, check windows and doors
10.30	To bed

Mistresses were advised to keep a check on the kitchen clock. Sometimes a frantic cook was tempted to adjust it with a broomstick!

Supper in the servants' hall.

SERVANTS' MEALS

One of the advantages of being a servant was that you were usually well fed. Servants' meals were simple, for example, cold meat from joints cooked for the dining room with hot vegetables, followed by a steamed pudding. They were prepared by a kitchenmaid.

The butler and housekeeper usually supervised servants' meals, except in very big houses where the higher rank servants ate separately. Either way, junior servants like scullerymaids and kitchen boys were served last and made to feel how unimportant they were.

THE DIRTY JOBS

A scullerymaid washing up.

In smaller households the kitchenmaid's job was combined with that of scullerymaid. She would have to do tedious jobs like scraping and pounding salt and sugar from great blocks, or chopping fat for suet, plucking poultry and cleaning fish.

She had to scrub the wooden tables, shelves and washing-up bowls. All day long there were pots and pans to scour and endless dishes to wash. Her hands were often soaked with harsh chemicals like washing soda and in winter they would be chapped and sore unless she looked after them very carefully.

POLISHING AND CLEANING

Servants were cheap to employ and while there were enough of them to share the work, it did not matter that there was a lot to do. There was always plenty of cleaning and polishing to be done. In this picture, servants are working hard to keep copper pans bright and polished. Kitchenmaids and scullerymaids used silver sand and ginger, or sand, vinegar and salt, to clean copper, rubbed on to the pans with their bare hands. They used pieces of lemon rind to rub sand into the corners of fancy moulds. Then they rinsed and polished them.

Cleaning copper pans.

THE KNIFE CLEANER

Most of the people working in the kitchen were women or girls. Some households employed a kitchen boy, sometimes called a 'knife boy' because an important part of his job was cleaning the knives each day. Knives were not made of stainless steel and would rust if they were simply washed and dried. They were rubbed on boards coated with brick dust. In the 1870s and 1880s various machines were made for cleaning knives. The knives were placed in the slots and a little emery powder or sand was poured into another hole. The handle turned brushes inside which polished the knives.

The knife cleaning machine.

REST

In a household with plenty of servants, a cook or kitchenmaid might expect a little time to herself in the evening, but a maid-of-all-work would still be busy at 11 o'clock. In big houses servants would have a sitting room, but it was not always comfortable. One handbook advised employers that there was no need for a sofa or armchairs in the servants' room, and rough matting would do for the floor. In smaller houses servants only had the kitchen to sit in.

Relaxing in the evening.

KITCHEN
SUPPLIES

There was a wide difference between what rich and poor people could afford to eat. In 1850, the family food bill for the year of Earl Fitzwilliam was £1,500 and that of a Suffolk labourer only £29. The middle-classes spent a sum somewhere between these two figures. Towns were growing as many workers moved from the country in search of work. More and more people bought all their food from shops, but the rich were able to use the freshest and best food from their own farms and gardens.

PROVISIONS

In town and country, Victorian cooks depended on shops for at least some of their provisions. Shopkeepers often let their customers have the goods they wanted and they paid their bills later. They hoped this would mean their customers would keep coming back for more goods. Towards the end of the century, big companies with shops all over the country began to be common. The Mazawattee Tea Company, for example, became a big company selling groceries. It had a number of shops that sold its own tea in sealed packets and all sorts of other goods as well. The company used advertising to persuade people to buy.

Victorian bills from local shops, Norfolk, 1890s.

PACKAGED FOOD

There were plenty of customers for shops in towns, but many of them were poor. Merchants, tempted to make their products cheaper, added chalk to flour, for example, or watered down milk. In 1856, Parliament was told that there were no foods or drinks which were not sometimes made impure before being sold. Food sold from open sacks or barrels could be tampered with at any time. Careful customers bought from shops they trusted and would test the goods once they got them home. For example, if chalk had been added, testing with lemon juice would make the chalk fizz. Once manufacturers started putting foods in sealed packets, customers could have more confidence that they were pure.

Goods in sealed packets and bottles.

TRAVELLING DEALERS

Many foods were delivered to the door. In country areas, travelling dealers called higglers would buy poultry, eggs and vegetables from people who had just a little produce and would sell this produce from door to door.

In towns, shops sent out deliveries to their regular customers. There were also 'tally-men' working in the suburbs of London and other cities. They had no shop but sold groceries from a cart. They let customers run up debts but collected weekly payments from them.

A higgler collecting poultry from a country home.

GARDENERS

Owners of large country houses picked fresh fruit and vegetables all year round from their kitchen gardens. When they stayed in their town houses they had hampers sent from the country. Gardeners were skilled at bringing on or slowing down particular crops, so there was always a good choice of the family's favourite things. Greenhouses were used to bring plants on faster and to grow crops used to a warmer climate. Some Victorian gardeners prided themselves on growing exotic fruits like pineapples, melons and grapes. The grapes in this picture are hanging in a storehouse.

They could be kept for up to three months if the stems were put in water containing charcoal to keep it fresh.

Grapes hanging in a storehouse.

A fruit house for keeping fruit fresh.

THE FRUIT STORE

Victorians had many ways of keeping foods fresh. A building like this fruit house was used for keeping apples and pears all year. Certain varieties were chosen because they were good keepers. The slatted shelves the fruit sat on let air flow round it and there was a stove which burned gently if there was a frost. Most households had a larder – a cupboard or room facing north for coolness with mesh on the window to keep flies out. Here they could keep dairy foods, cold meat and cooked dishes.

THE KITCHEN GARDEN

Country workers were very poorly paid. The lucky ones were able to grow some of what they needed in the gardens around their cottages. They grew vegetables and herbs, kept chickens if they could afford to, and maybe even a pig. Herbs were important for flavouring cheap, dull foods like dumplings, suet puddings and lard. Fresh vegetables – onions, carrots, turnips, cabbages, kale, potatoes – made a poor diet much healthier. They were usually eaten simply boiled.

The cottage garden at Gressenhall, Norfolk.

VICTORIAN MEALS

Well-off people spent a lot of money on their food and mealtimes were an important part of daily life. The poor had little money and less time to spend over a meal than the rich. The middle-classes ate hearty breakfasts, light lunches and enormous dinners. It was fashionable to have guests for dinner often, perhaps once a week. Dinner time became later during Victoria's reign, so more was eaten at tea time to fill the gap.

A WORKING MAN'S MEAL

This working man looks quite satisfied with his dinner. Very likely he is eating a little meat cooked together with potatoes or dumplings. We can imagine that for breakfast he had bread with bacon or treacle and, for lunch, bread with cheese or cold meat. Bread was very expensive during the 1830s. When very poor people could not afford bread, they might breakfast on flour mixed with hot water and a little fat. Tea, drunk with plenty of sugar, was popular and cheered people up, but it was not very nourishing.

Working-class family, 1858.

RECIPE BOOKS

Mistresses liked their cooks to work from recipe books so that they could repeat dishes or change them for the family's tastes. *Mrs Beeton's Book of Household Management*, which first appeared as a book in 1861, was one of the most useful. As well as giving hundreds of recipes, she explained how to buy, keep and serve food, how housework should be done, and the duties of servants. She gave menus listing suitable dishes for meals all year round, not forgetting picnics and ball suppers. Few middle-class mistresses managed without the advice of Mrs Beeton.

One of Mrs Beeton's cookery books.

DINNER GUESTS

Middle and upper-class Victorians liked to ask guests to come for dinner. This was when the cook really earned her salary. A dinner for 6 people in June would include the following dishes:

> Green pea soup. Baked sole with herbs.
> Stewed trout.
> Calf's liver and bacon. Rissoles.
> Roast saddle of lamb and salad. Calf's head.
> Vegetables.
> Roast ducks. Vol-au-vent of strawberries and cream.
> Strawberry tartlets. Lemon blancmange.
> Baked gooseberry pudding.

A different wine was served with each course and different plates and cutlery used. A servant in the dining room rang a bell in the kitchen to tell the cook when to send up each course.

A Victorian dining room laid for dinner.

VICTORIAN DISHES

When they had not invited guests for a meal, middle-class Victorians ate fairly plainly. Even so, their dinners were usually of three courses. First there was soup and fish. Then the main course which included two sorts of meat with vegetables, followed by a pudding. Fish, like vegetables and fruit, had to be eaten during the right season, so cooks needed to know they could buy cod or smelts in the winter, salmon or mackerel in the summer. This page from Mrs Beeton's cookbook showed cooks how to serve fish dishes.

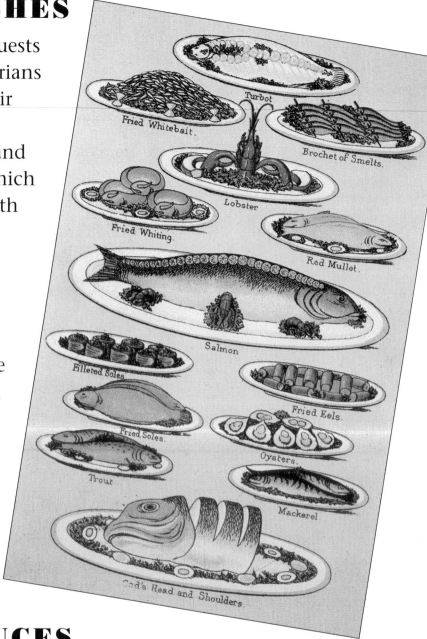

A page from Mrs Beeton's cookbook.

SOUPS AND SAUCES

There were soups or sauces served at every meal. Kitchenmaids had to learn which sauces matched which foods. A simple gravy took several hours to make. Finely chopped meat was stewed, strained and flavoured with herbs and seasonings. After cooling, the fat was removed and the gravy reheated for serving. Another lengthy task was making soup smooth by pushing it through a fine cloth held between two kitchenmaids. Clear soups and smooth, delicately flavoured sauces were taken as one of the signs of a good cook.

A Wedgewood and Bentley Queensware tureen.

SPECIAL DIETS

Victorians ate heavily but they believed that their usual diet was not suitable for everybody. A cook needed to be able to plan and cook meals for people whose digestions were not so strong, such as invalids and children.

Some Victorians thought children should never eat fresh bread or cake. Jelly was considered nourishing invalid food if it was made by boiling calves' feet instead of using isinglass. The feet were boiled for six hours, and the top was skimmed all the time, then the liquid was strained through a jelly bag and left to set in a jelly mould. Flavoured and coloured, jelly was also nice for a dinner party. Blancmange, made of isinglass or arrowroot and milk was more quickly made for both invalids and children.

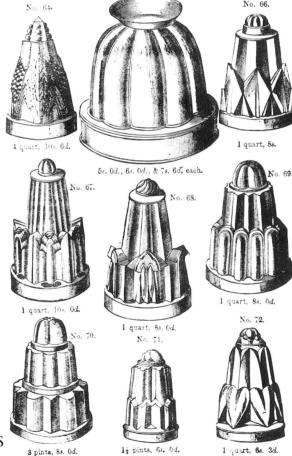

Moulds for jelly or blancmange.

NEW WAYS IN THE KITCHEN

By the end of the nineteenth century buying, storing and cooking food was cheaper and easier than it had ever been. Victorians were very inventive. Some became very rich by selling new convenience foods or gadgets to make work in the kitchen easier. A few politicians and religious leaders encouraged changes which would improve the diet of the poor. The new tinned and frozen foods and convenient gas cookers all helped the poor to eat better.

GAS COOKERS

Gas cookers were first used in the kitchens of hotels, but they were too big for people's homes. By the 1880s there were many styles of gas cooker for sale. The one in this picture has a water boiler on the side, like some of the old coal-fired kitcheners. Gas cookers were much easier to use than kitcheners but some people were suspicious that the gas would spoil the food. The gas companies began to hire out gas cookers and more people tried them. Poorer people started using them when slot meters were attached, so they were not afraid of large bills.

Advertisement for a gas cooker, 1889.

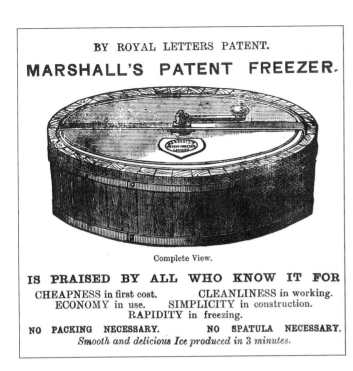

BY ROYAL LETTERS PATENT.

MARSHALL'S PATENT FREEZER.

Complete View.

IS PRAISED BY ALL WHO KNOW IT FOR

CHEAPNESS in first cost.   CLEANLINESS in working.
ECONOMY in use.   SIMPLICITY in construction.
RAPIDITY in freezing.

NO PACKING NECESSARY.   NO SPATULA NECESSARY.
Smooth and delicious Ice produced in 3 minutes.

FREEZING FOOD

Could you live without ice-cream? Well-off Victorians did not have to. Blocks of ice could be bought from an ice man in most towns. Cooks used them for keeping food fresh and some cooks had special ice-chests. To make ice-cream you could use one of the patent ice-making machines like the one in the picture. It would be packed with ice and salt, or special freezing crystals. The inner drum contained the ice-cream mixture and the handle turned a paddle to make it freeze smoothly.

IMPORTING MEAT

Cooks had been using ice to make special puddings even before Victoria's reign. Freezing food to keep it fresh was not successful until the 1870s. This picture shows how cargoes of pork and beef were brought from America to London and Glasgow in Scotland. They were carried in steamships with refrigerated holds. In 1880 a cargo of frozen Australian beef and mutton was unloaded from the S.S. *Strathleven* and sold in London. Importing meat from abroad meant prices fell and poor people could buy good meat more regularly.

STEAM-LIGHTER RECEIVING CARGO OF MEAT

The meat trade.

CONVENIENCE FOODS

Unless they were able to preserve food by salting, pickling or cooking with sugar, early Victorian cooks had to use everything in season. In 1857, the French chemist, Louis Pasteur discovered that bacteria caused food to spoil. After this, attempts to can food began to be successful. By the end of the century there was a huge variety of tinned foods to choose from. Some of the tinned meat was not very nice but it was cheap. Other convenience foods were invented, giving the cook quick ways to make gravy, jelly, blancmange and custard.

Tinned foods.

Powders to make quick meals.

FOOD PROCESSING

This is an early food processor. It could be used for chopping suet or vegetables, or for mixing. The drum went round when the handle was turned and the chopping blade went up and down to cut up the food. Servants were not always pleased when their employers bought new gadgets. The makers often advertised them as 'servants' friends' but they were used to doing tasks to a high standard by hand. At the end of the century it became more difficult to keep servants. There were other jobs in factories and offices for young women which gave them more money and freedom. Soon the middle-classes were going to be glad of the gadgets for themselves.

Early food processor.

A teenager cooking.

A KITCHEN TODAY

The next time you are cooking, try to imagine what it was really like working in a Victorian kitchen. Advertisers today sometimes like to make us think of Victorian kitchens as cosy, cheerful places where lots of wholesome food was cooked. In fact many kitchens were dismal, nearly impossible to keep clean, and the food to be cooked was expensive and sometimes of poor quality. We expect that preparing the food for a family can be something done in the time left over after other activities. In Victorian times, it was full-time work for a team of people.

TIME LINE

	BC	AD 0		500	
		43		410	
				'THE DARK AGES'	
CELTS		ROMAN BRITAIN		ANGLO-SAXONS	VIKINGS

EARLY 1800s

1802 Closed iron range invented by George Bodley, Devon.

1808 Mrs Rundell's cookery book *A New System of Domestic Cookery* published.

1812 Food preserved in handmade tins by Donkin, Hall and Gamble.

1824 John Robison of Edinburgh, Scotland, first experimented with cooking with gas.

1830s

Matches invented.

1837 Queen Victoria came to the throne.

1840s

1841 Kitchens of the Reform Club, London, converted to gas.

1845 Eliza Acton's *Modern Cookery for Private Families* published.

1845 Wages at their lowest for 100 years.

1847 Cochin chickens brought to Britain, encouraging a craze for chicken keeping.

1850s

1850 Joseph Sharp, Southampton, offered a gas cooker for sale.

1854 Process for extracting cornflour invented by Polsen.

1856 Ice-filled refrigerator with circulating air invented.

1066

MIDDLE AGES

1485

NORMANS

TUDORS

STUARTS

GEORGIANS

VICTORIANS

20TH CENTURY

1860s

1860 First Adulteration of Foods Act passed by Parliament, allowing customers to get foods analyzed if they were prepared to pay for it.

1861 Mrs Beeton's *Book of Household Management* published.

1865 Cattle disease put price of fresh meat and dairy foods very high.

1866 Australian 'boiled mutton' in tins imported.

Process of condensing milk invented.

1869 Margarine invented.

1870s

1873 Typhoid epidemic in London, spread by one person working in a dairy.

1875 Sale of Food and Drugs Act passed by parliament, greatly improved the quality of food.

1877 First refrigerated ship docked in London, with 400 sheep and 1,200 quarters of beef.

1880s

1882 Kent's Rotary Knife Cleaner invented.

1886 H.J. Heinz brought sample tinned food to Fortnum and Masons, London.

International Electric and Gas Exhibiton, Crystal Palace, London.

1890s

1890 Marie J. Sugg's *The Art of Cooking by Gas* published.

1895 Cooking by electricity demonstrated by Margaret Fairclough.

1900s

1901 Queen Victoria died.

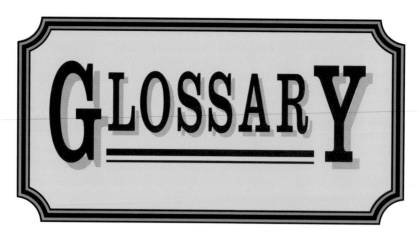

GLOSSARY

Bacteria Tiny organisms.

Blancmange A milky jelly made in a mould.

Butler Senior male servant in charge of the serving of meals.

Chef Usually the most important cook in the kitchen.

Course A group of dishes served together as part of a meal.

Dripping The fat that drips from roasting meat.

Emery powder Powder used for smoothing and polishing.

Employer A person or business that takes on people to work.

Flues Chimney pipes.

Gadget Tool made to do a particular job.

Higgler To higgle or haggle means to wrangle over a price. A higgler sold goods at the best price he could get.

Isinglass A type of gelatine taken from fish.

Kitchenmaid A servant who helped the cook.

Luncheon A light meal eaten in the middle of the day.

Poultry Birds like chickens, ducks and geese.

Privileges Special benefits given to people.

Professed Fully trained.

Range A large coal-burning stove with one or more ovens.

Rissoles Little rounds of cooked meat, often coated and fried.

Salary A regular payment made by an employer.

Scullery A room where washing-up and other kitchen cleaning jobs were done.

Smelts Small silvery fish.

Soles A kind of flat fish.

Suet Hard fat from meat, used in steamed puddings

Turpentine A sticky liquid made from tree gum.

BOOKS TO READ

General:

Davies, J. *The Victorian Kitchen* (BBC Enterprises, 1989)

Drury, E. *The Butler's Pantry Book* (section on the work of the cook and kitchenmaids pages 133–160), (A & C Black, 1981)

Other books for children:

Chamberlain, E. *Everyday Life in the Nineteenth Century* (Macdonald Educational, 1983)

Chaney, L. *Breakfast* (A & C Black, 1992)

Chaney, L. *Investigating Food in History* (The National Trust, 1992)

Lawrie, J. *Pot Luck: Cooking and Recipes from the Past* (A & C Black, 1991)

PLACES TO VISIT

ENGLAND

Berkshire: Museum of English Rural Life, Reading. Tel: 0734 318660

Cambridgeshire: Cambridge and County Folk Museum, 2/3 Castle Street, CB3 OAQ. Tel: 0223 355159

Cornwall: Lanhydrock House, Lanhydrock Park, Bodmin, PL30 5AD. Tel: 0208 73320

London: Science Museum, Exhibition Road, SW7 2DD. Tel: 071 938 8000

North Cornwall Museum and Gallery, The Clease, Camelford, Cornwall. Tel: 0840 212954

Norfolk: Holkham Hall, Wells-next-the-Sea. Tel: 0328 710227

Strangers' Hall, Charing Cross, Norwich, NR2 4AL. Tel: 0603 667229

Surrey: Clandon Park, West Clandon, Guildford, GU4 7RQ. Tel: 0483 222482

Sussex: Brighton Pavilion, Brighton, BN1 1UE. Tel: 0273 603005

Warwickshire: Charlecote Park, Stratford, Warwickshire. Tel: 0789 470472

Yorkshire: Castle Museum, York, YO1 2RUY. Tel: 0904 653611

Ryedale Folk Museum, Hutton-le-Hole, N. Yorkshire, YO6 6UA. Tel: 07515367

NORTHERN IRELAND

Castle Ward, Co. Down, N. Ireland. Tel: 0396 881204

WALES

Erddig, Clwyd, Wales, LL11 1BF. Tel: 0978 358916

Wallington, Cambo, Morpeth, NE61 4AR. Tel: 067 074 283

Welsh Folk Museum, St. Fagans, Cardiff, CF5 6XB. Tel: 0222 569441

INDEX